Bruges,

Chester &

Ampleforth College

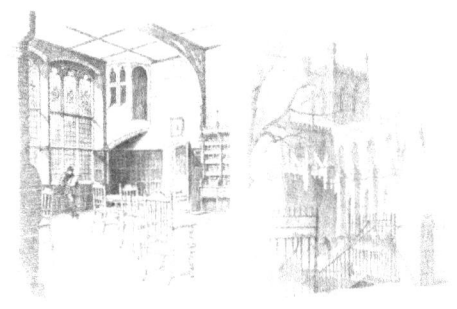

By

Joseph Pike

BRUGES

A SKETCH-BOOK
BY JOSEPH PIKE

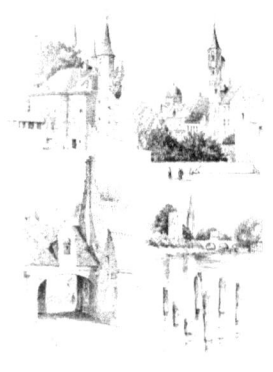

1922

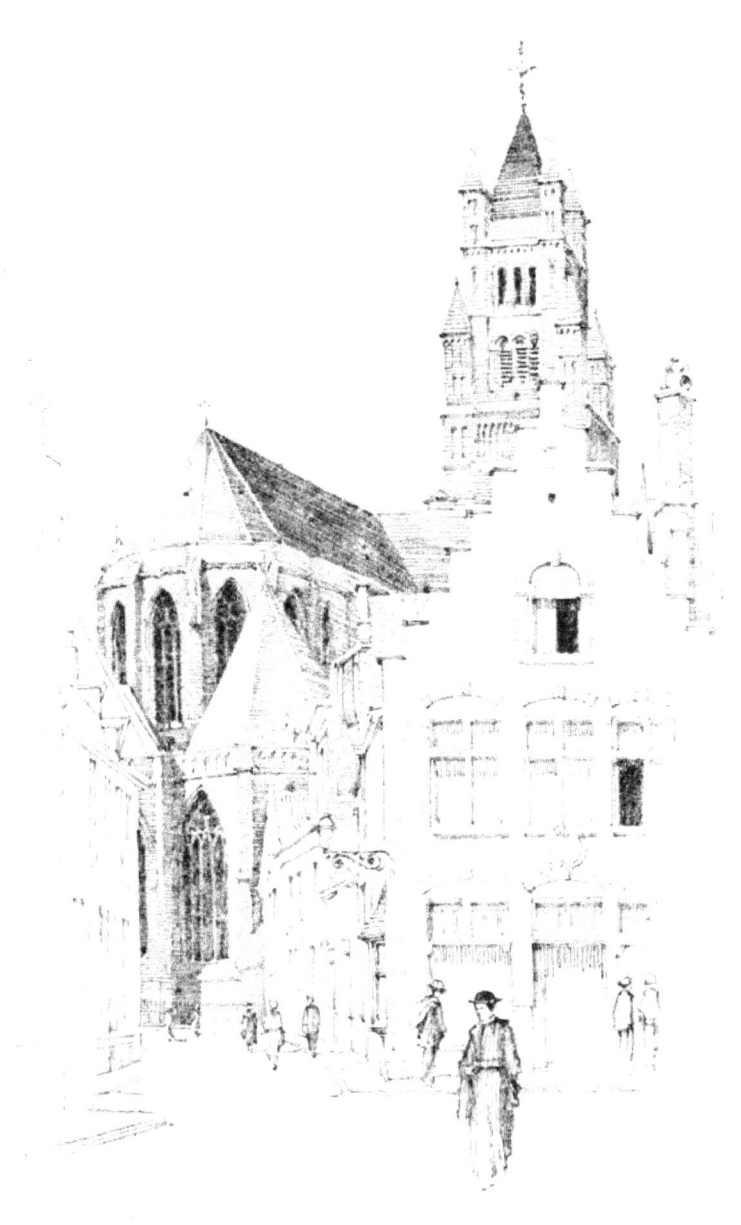

CATHEDRALE S. SAUVEUR
FROM PLACE SIMON STEVIN

CATHEDRALE ST. SAUVEUR FROM PLACE SIMON STEVIN

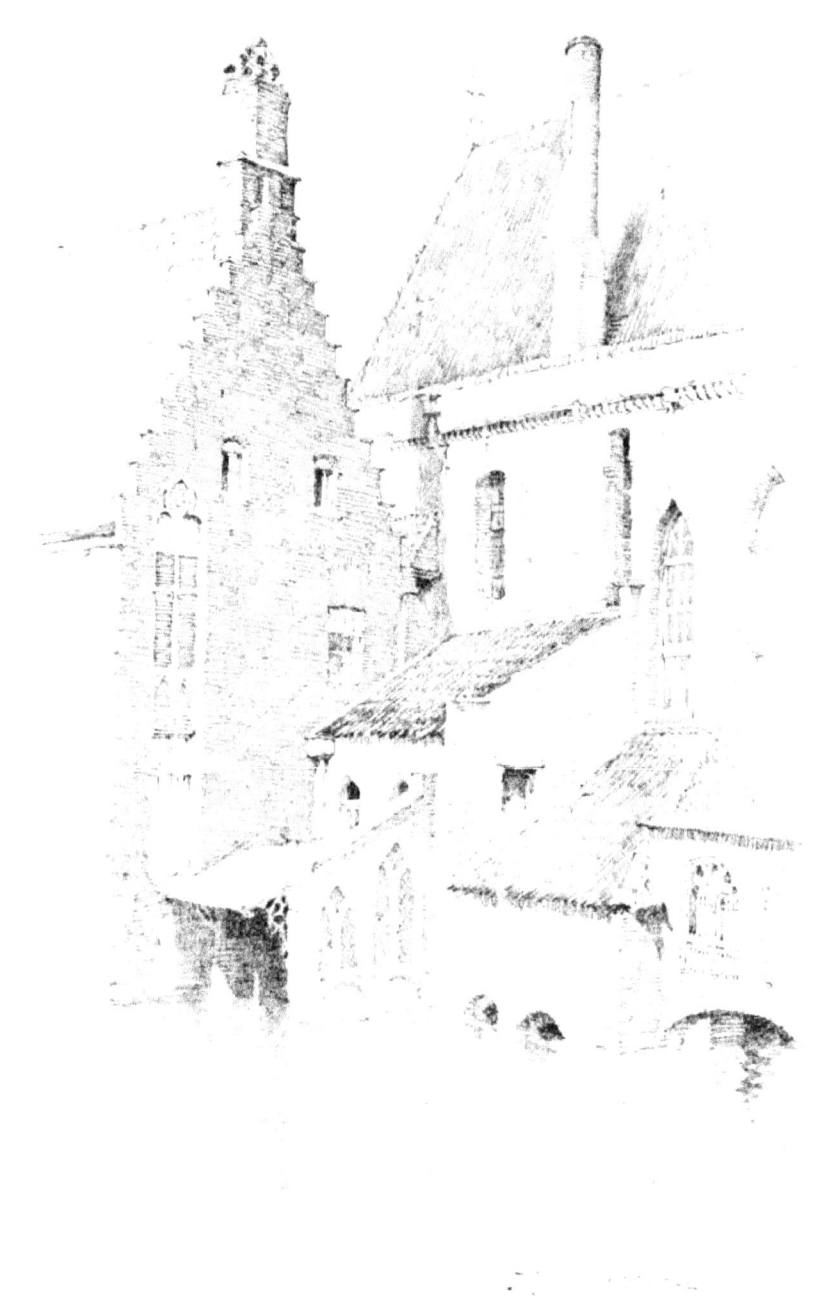

ST. JOHN'S HOSPITAL

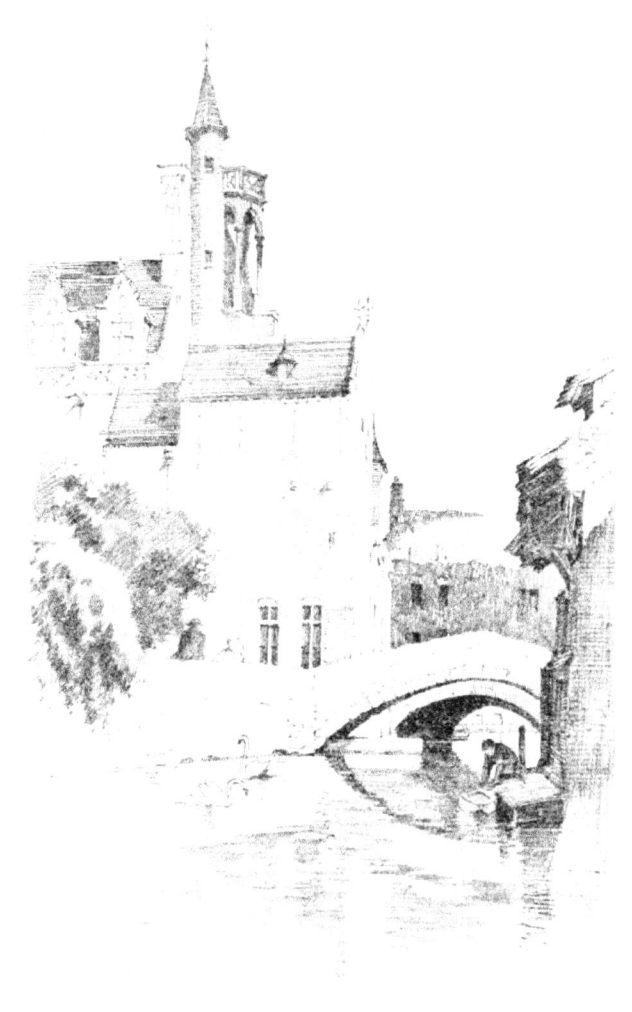

HOTEL GRUUTHUSE AND PONT ST BONIFACE

HOTEL GRUUTHUSE AND PONT
ST BONIFACE

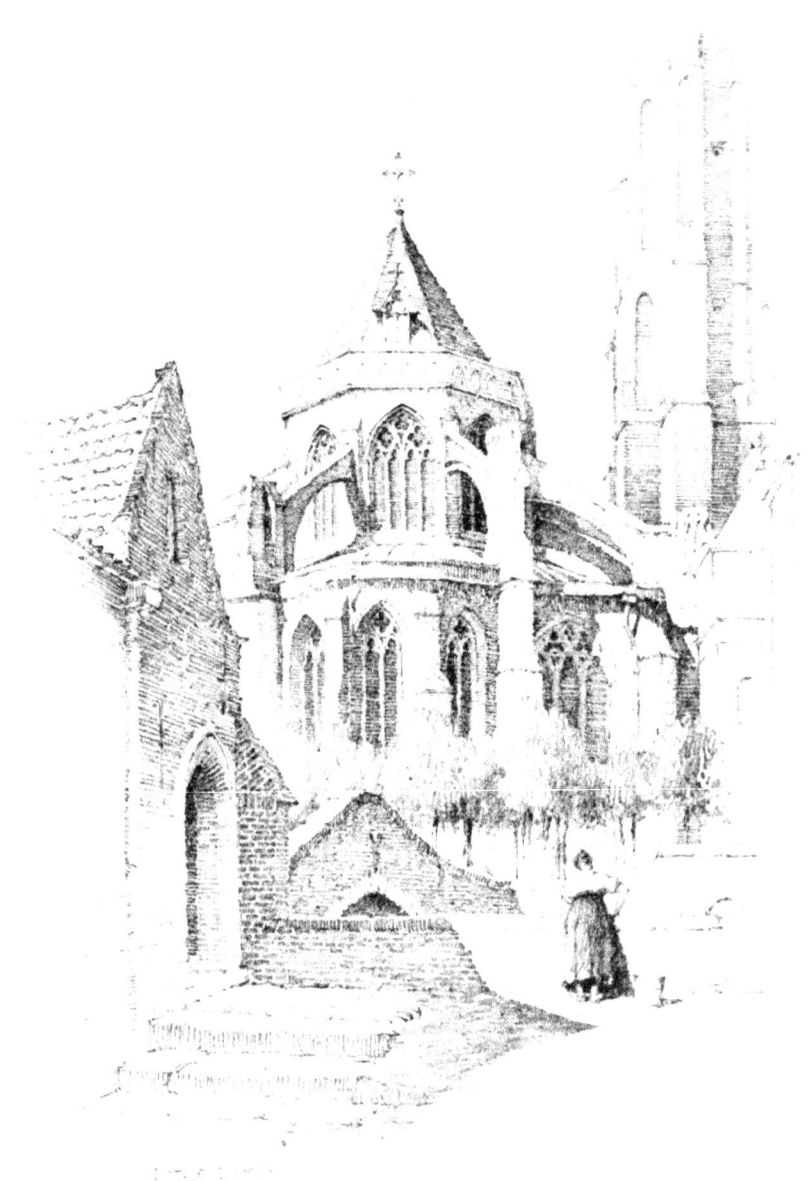

NOTRE DAME

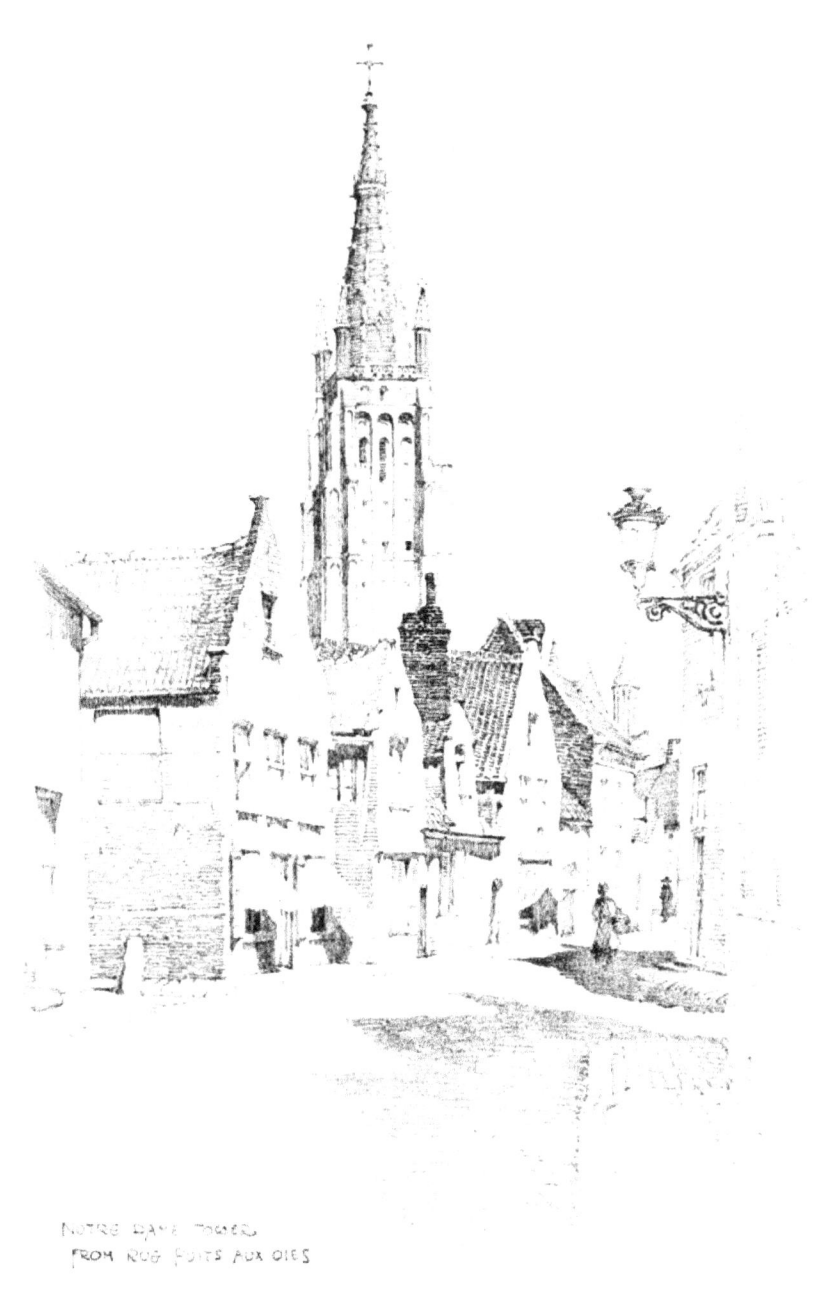

NOTRE DAME TOWER FROM RUE
PUITS AUX OIES

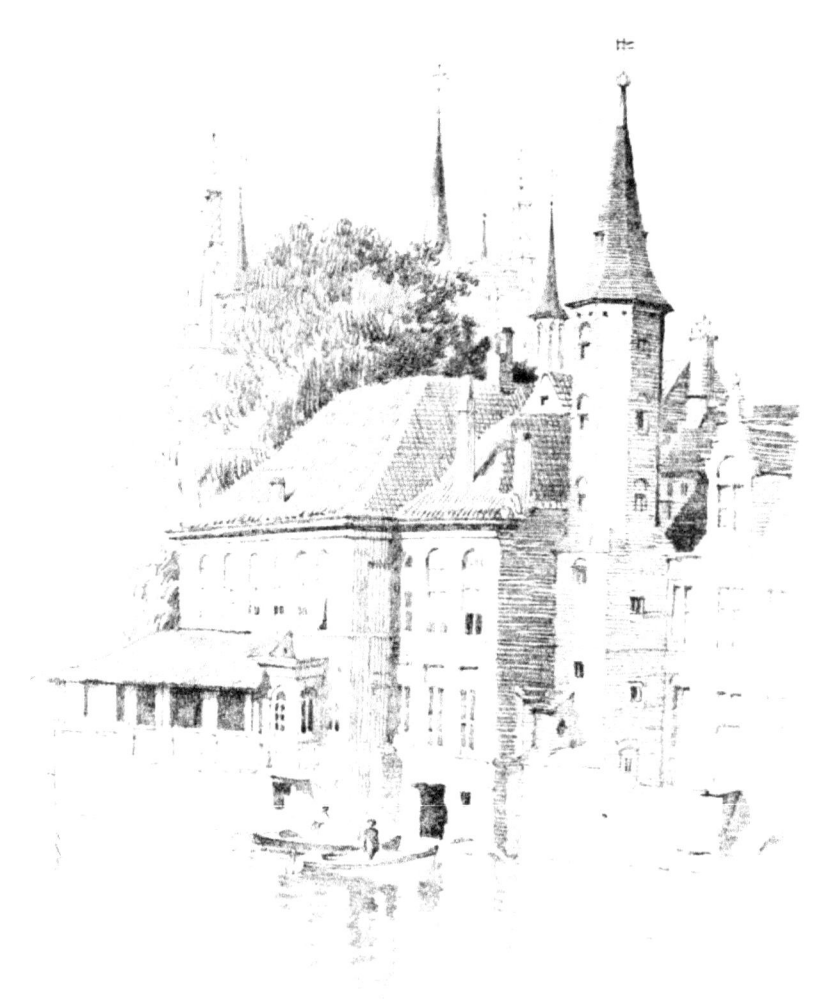

THE QUAI DU ROSAIRE

QUAI DU ROSAIRE

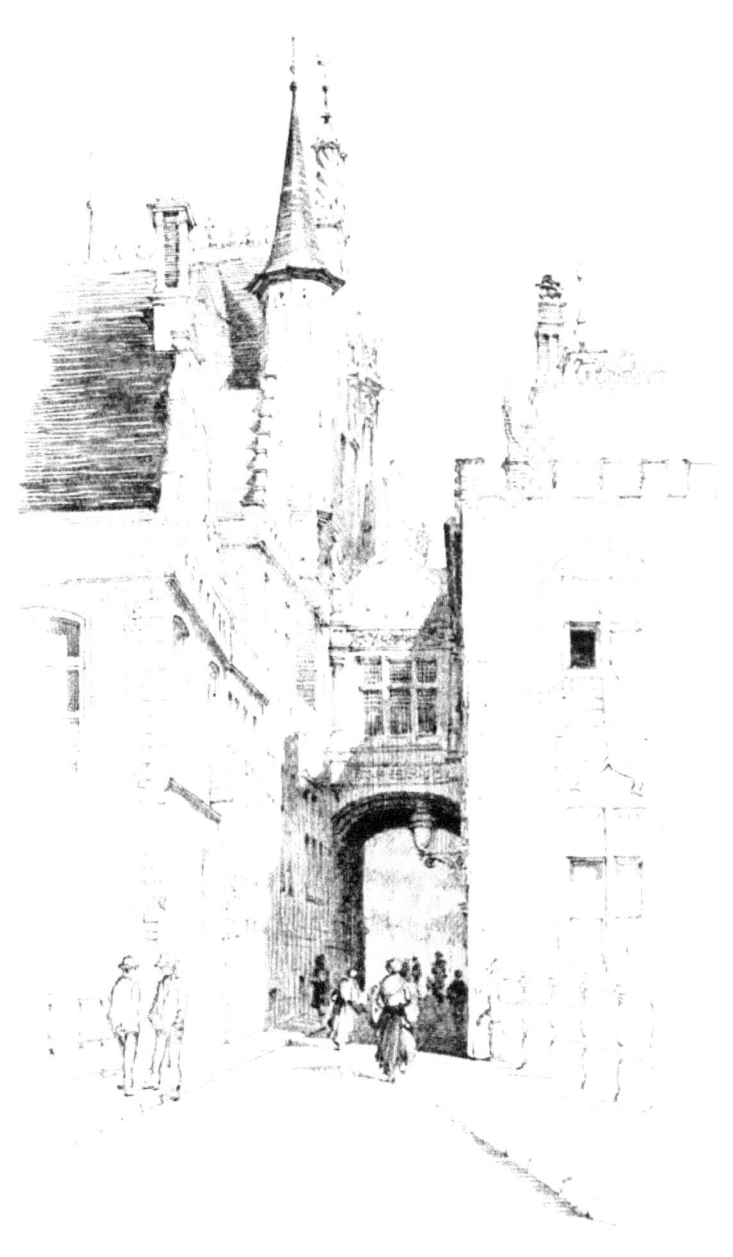

RUE DE L'ANE AVEUGLE

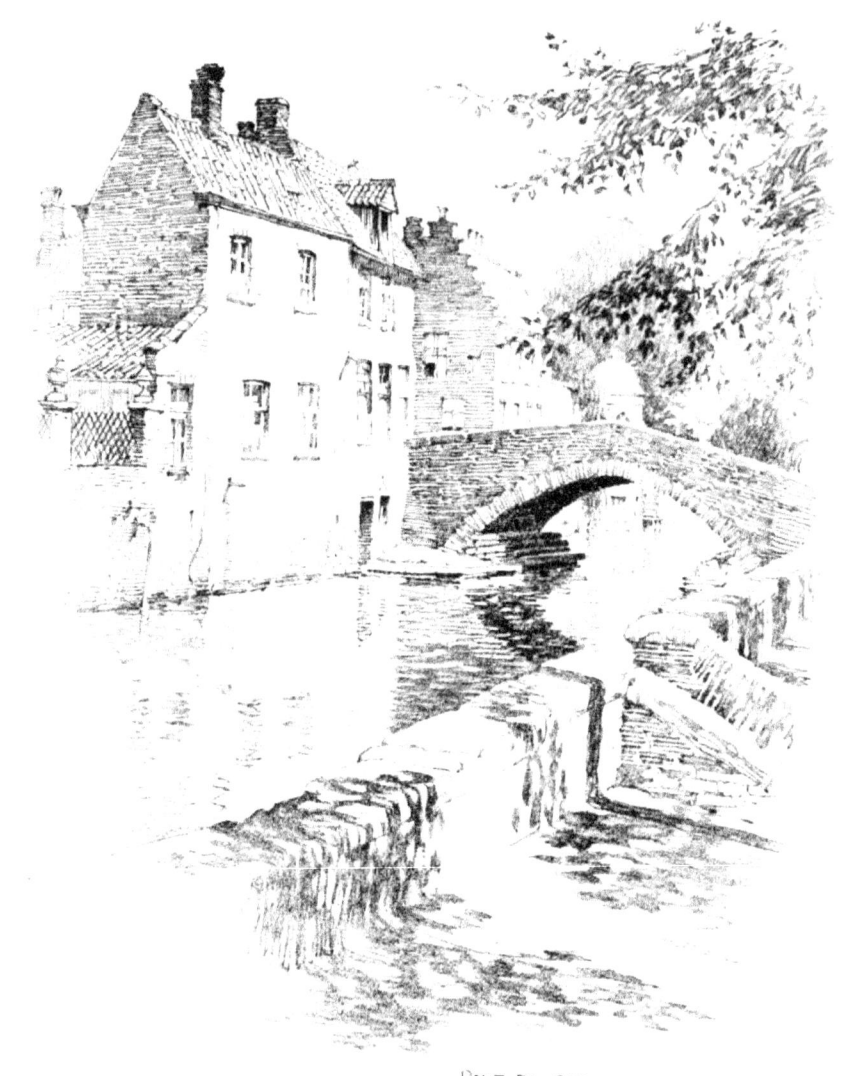

PONT DU CHEVAL

PONT DU CHEVAL

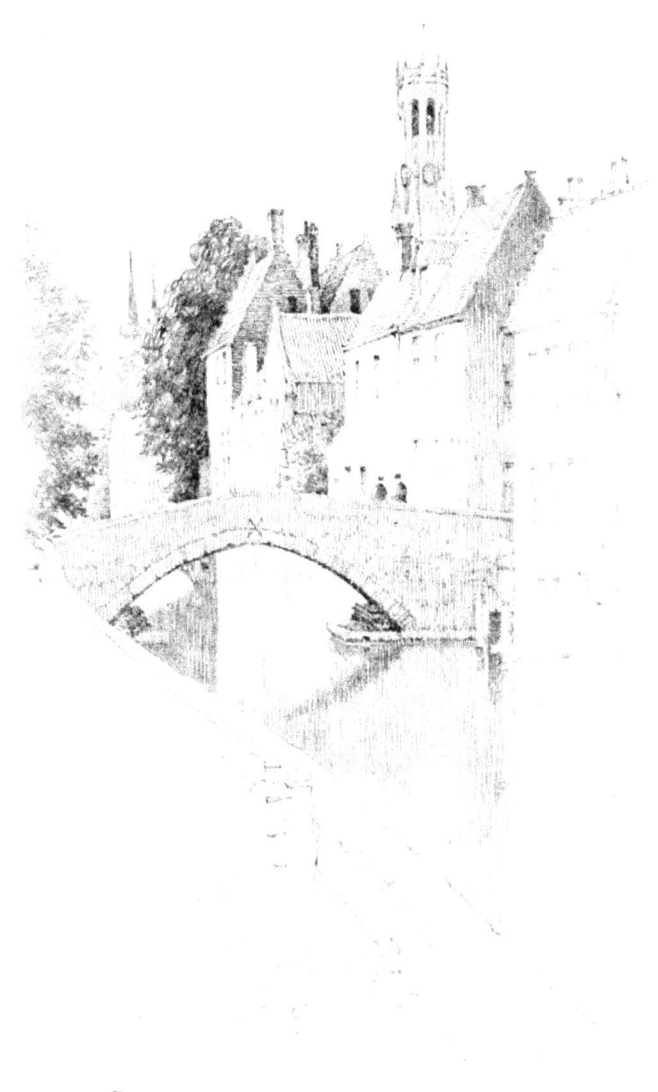

THE QUAI VERT

THE QUAI VERT

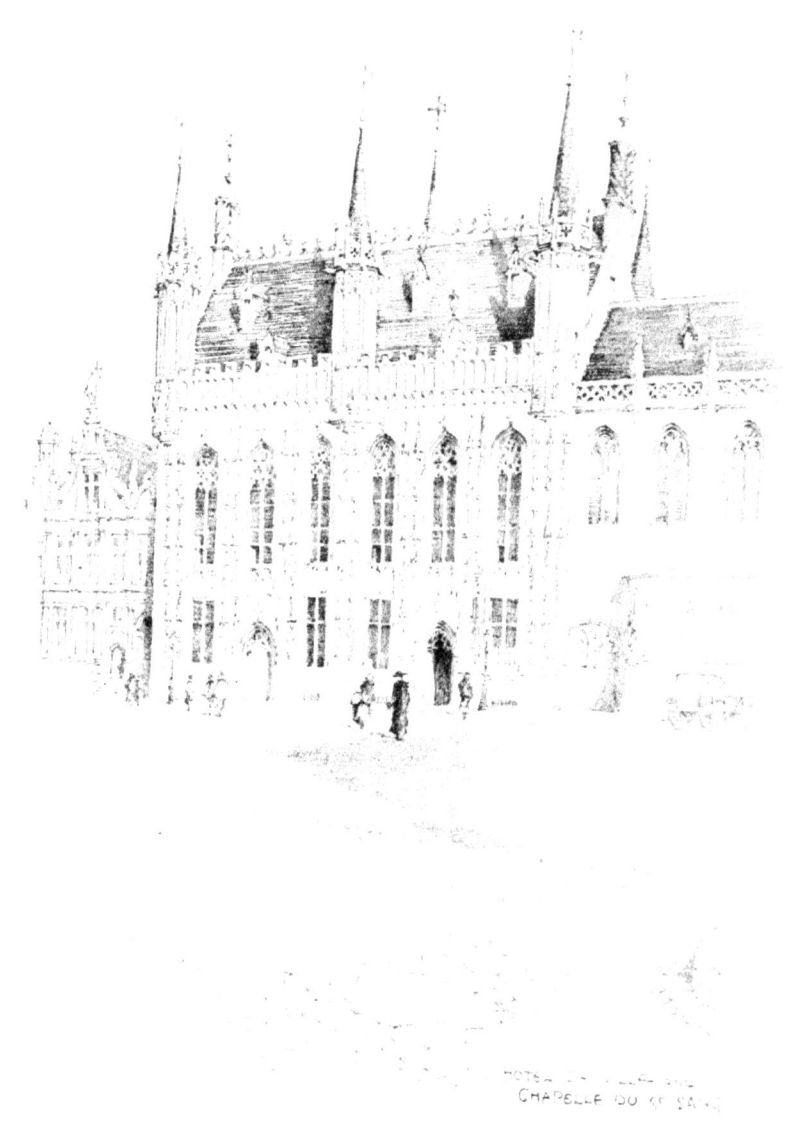

HOTEL DE VILLE AND CHAPELLE
DU ST. SANG

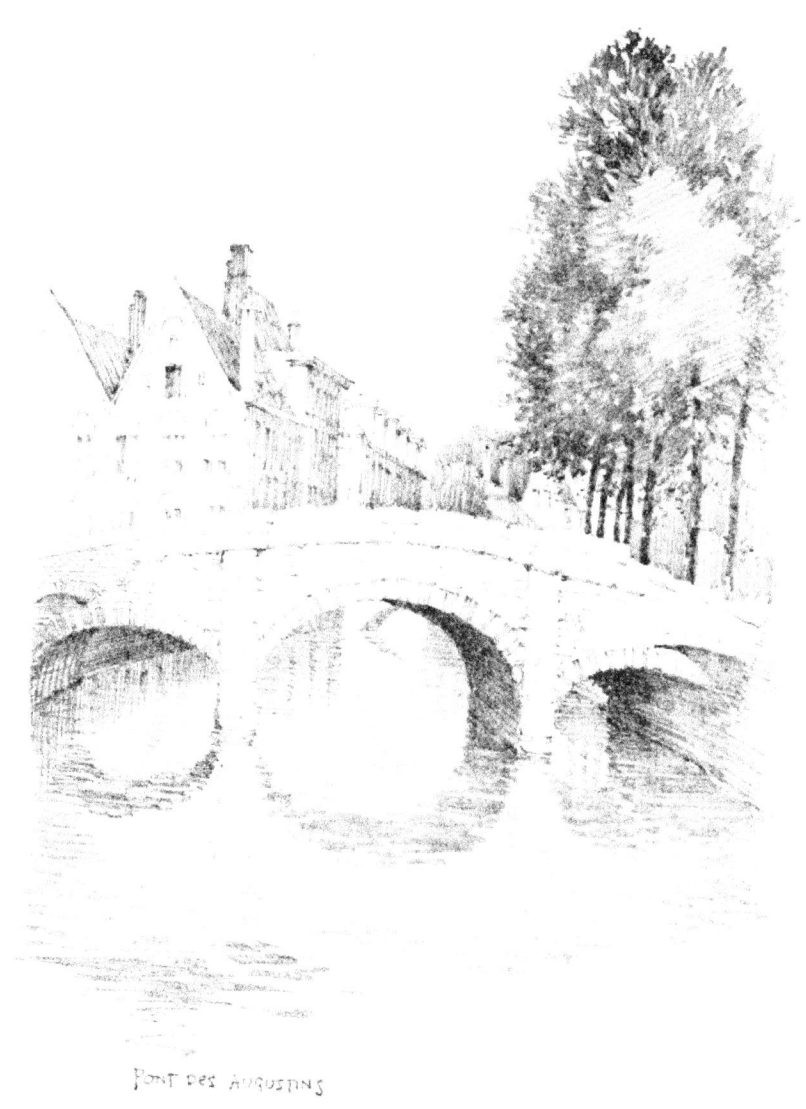

PONT DES AUGUSTINS

PONT DES AUGUSTINS

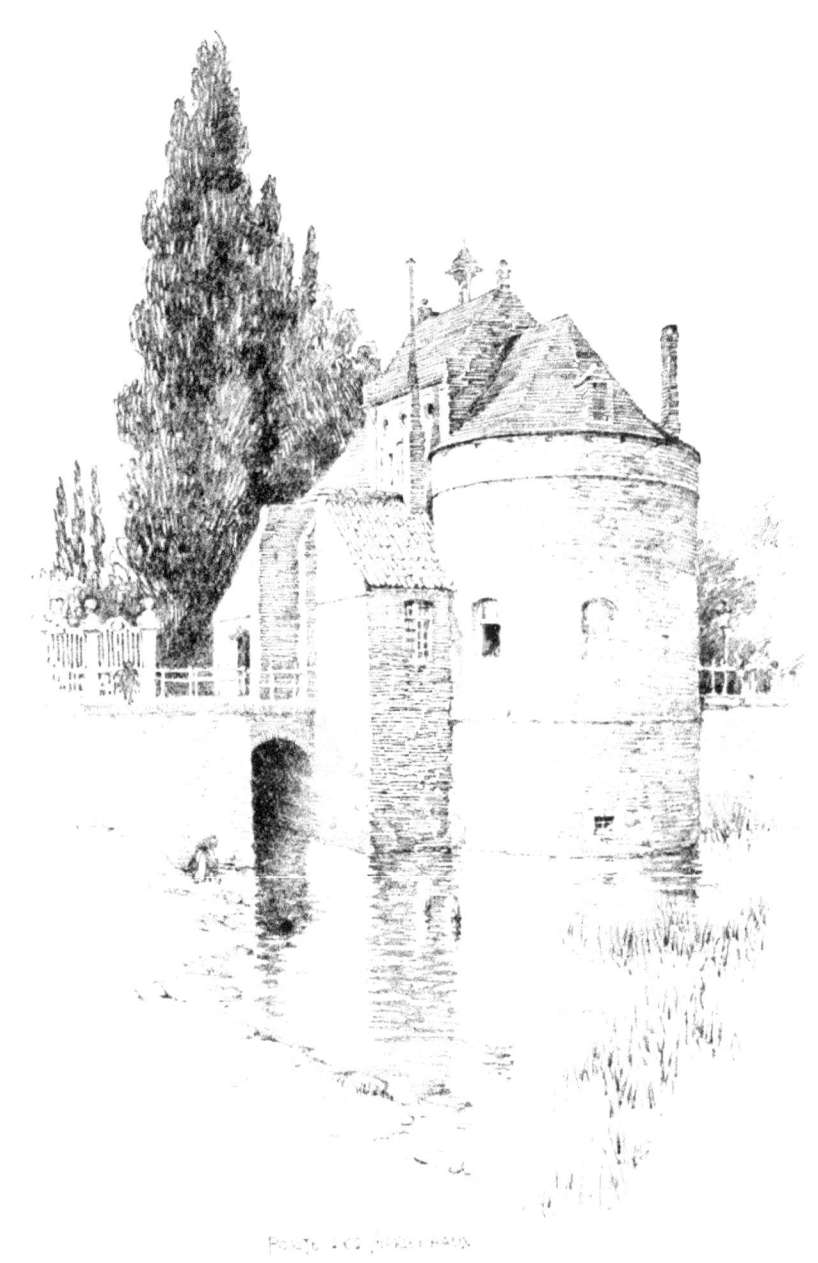

PORTE DE MARECHAUX

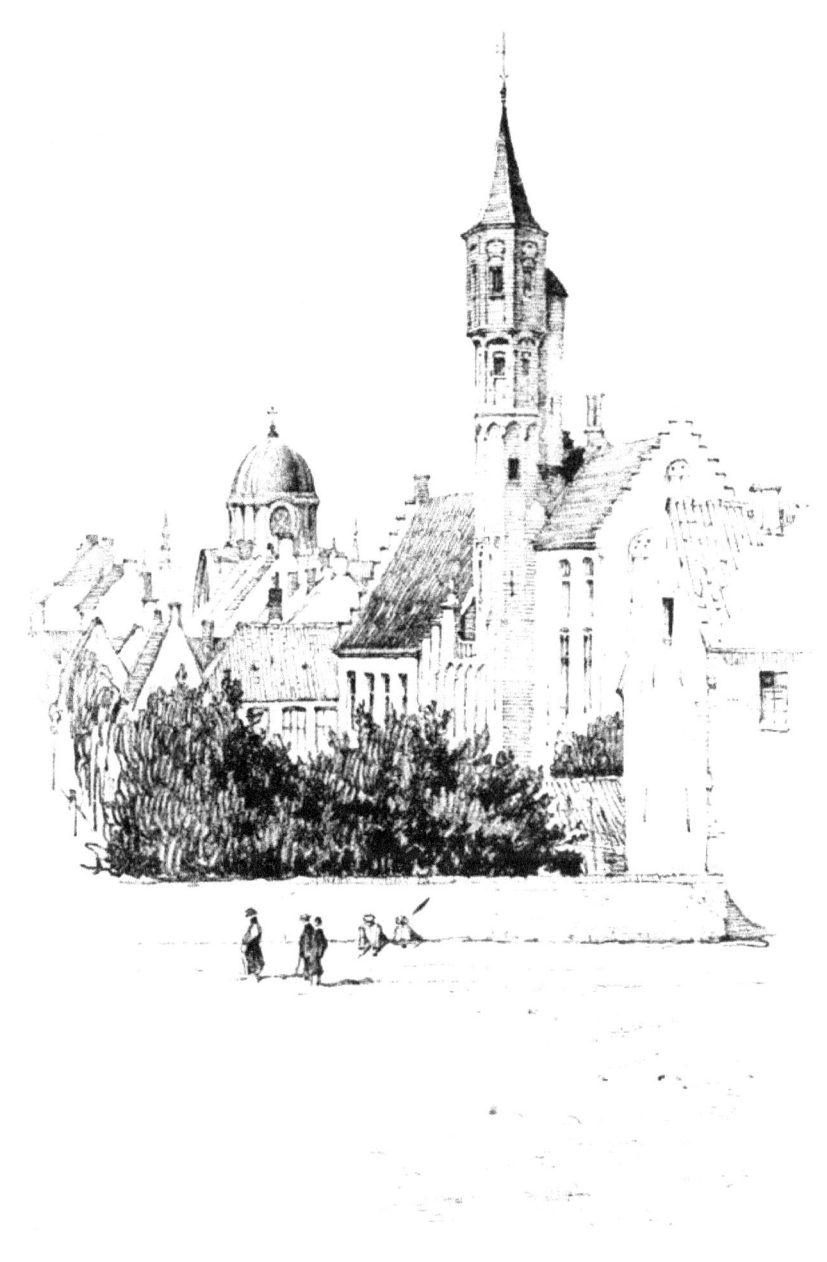

TOUR ST SEBASTIAN
AND THE ENGLISH CONVENT

TOUR ST. SEBASTIAN AND THE ENGLISH CONVENT

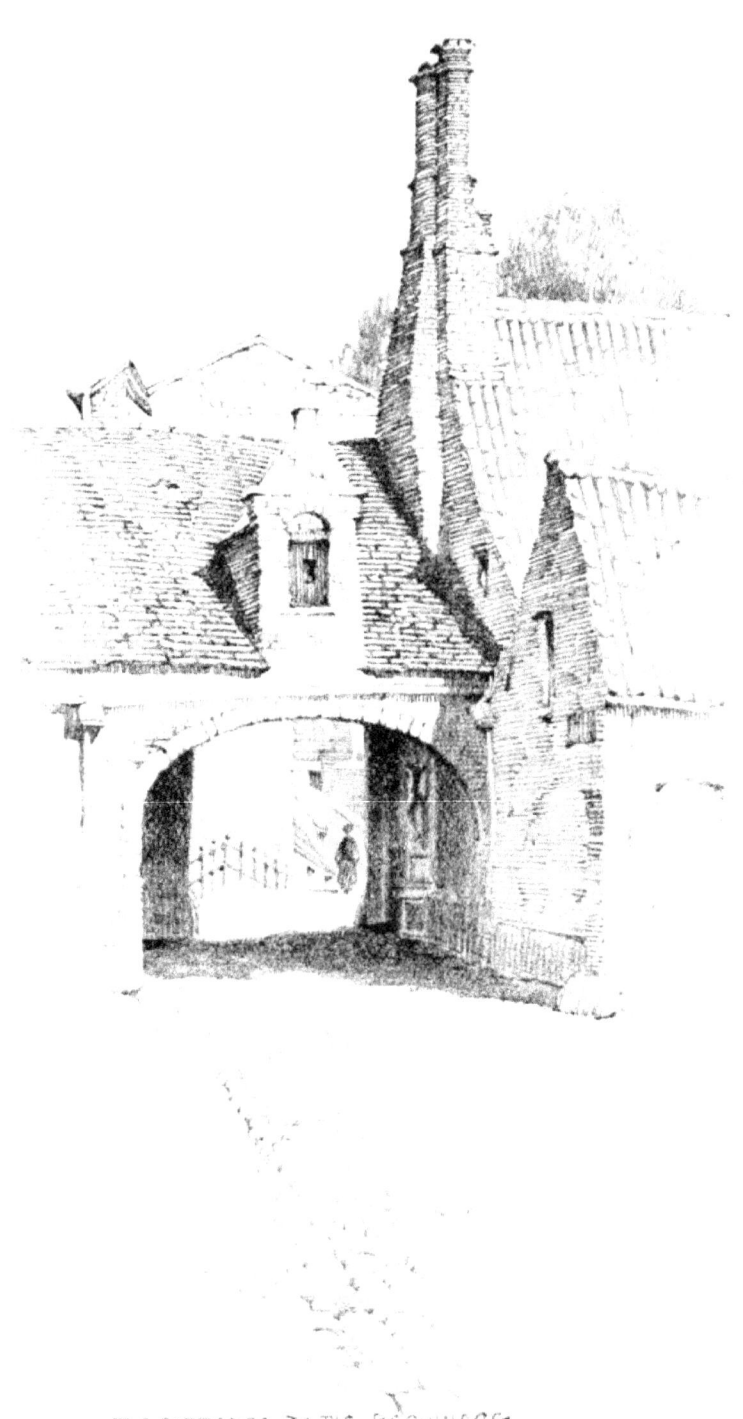

THE ENTRANCE TO THE BEGUINAGE

THE ENTRANCE TO THE BEGUINAGE

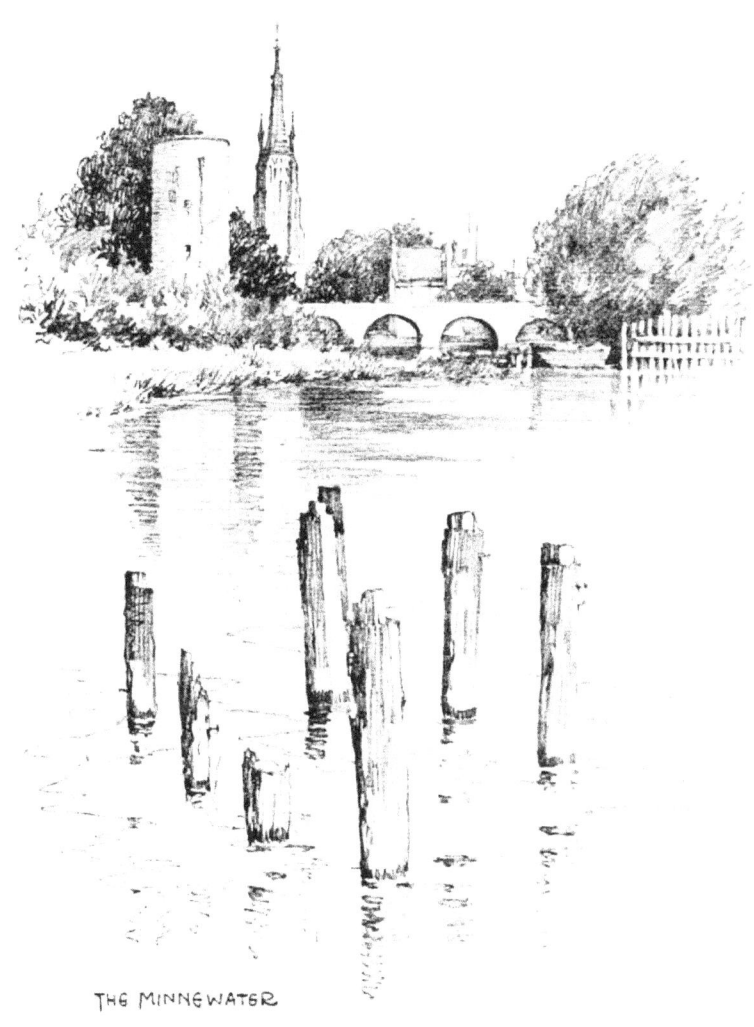

THE MINNEWATER

THE MINNEWATER.

Chester

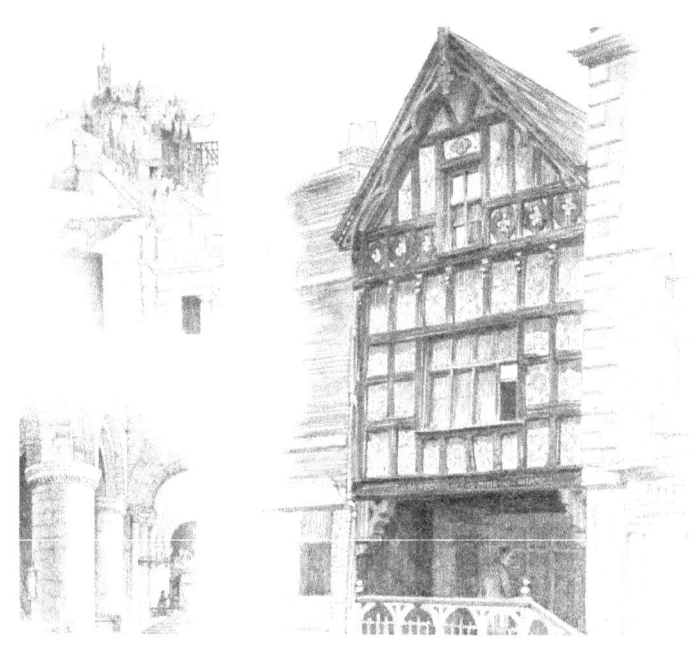

A Sketch-
Book By
Joseph Pike

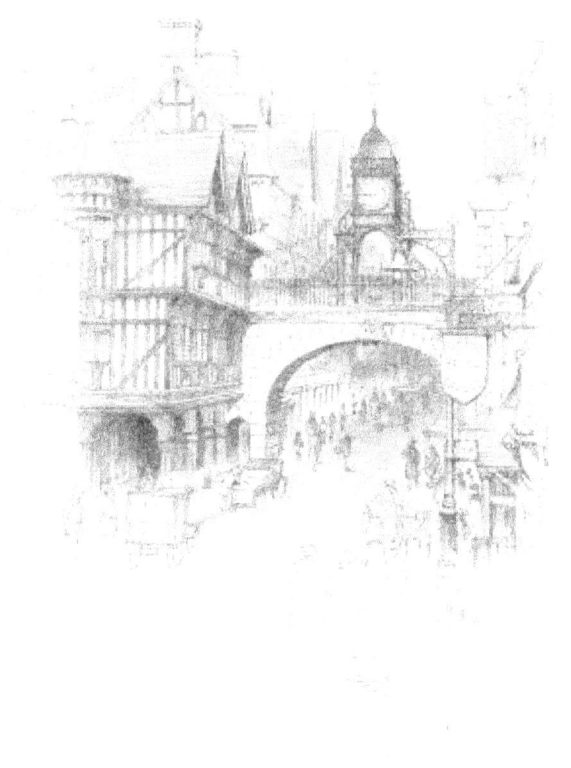

FOREGATE STREET.

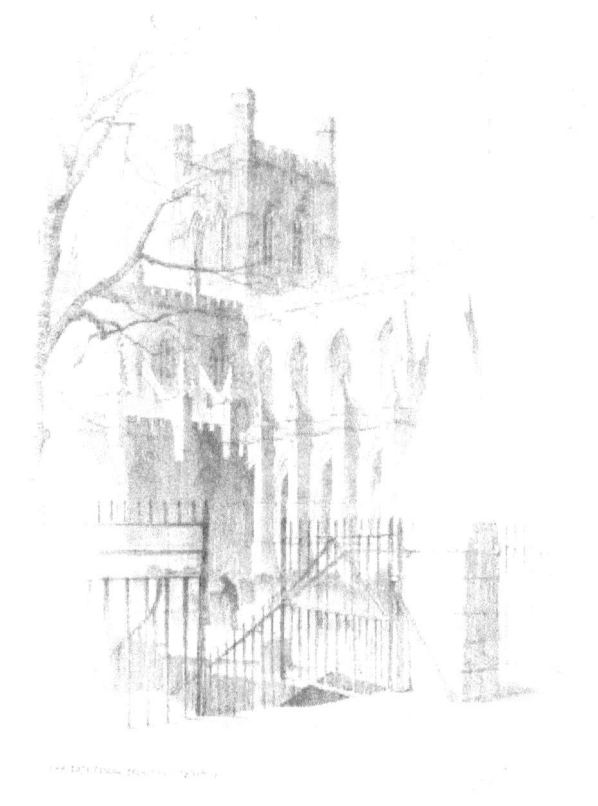

THE CATHEDRAL FROM THE CITY WALLS.

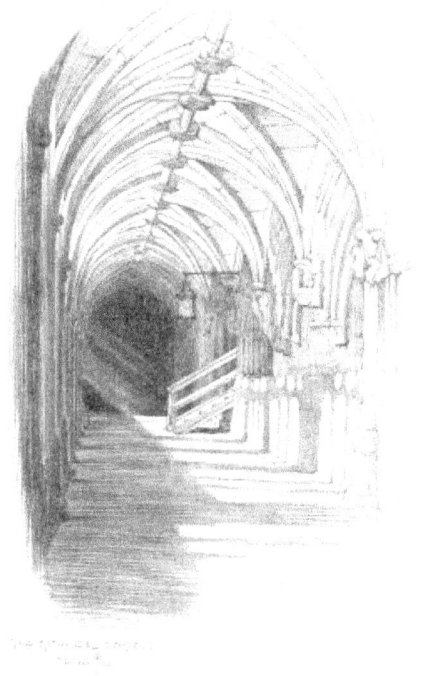

THE CATHEDRAL CLOISTERS.

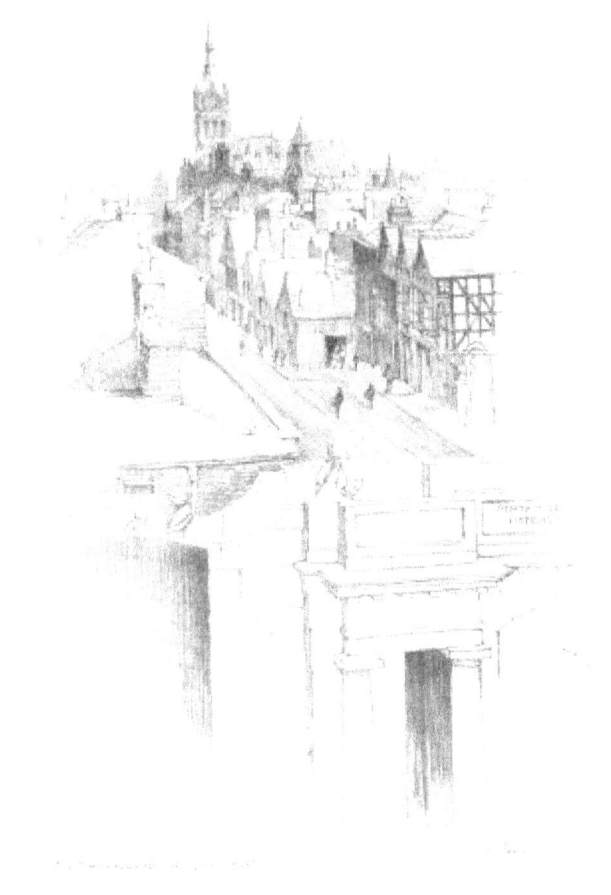

THE TOWN HALL AND NORTHGATE STREET.

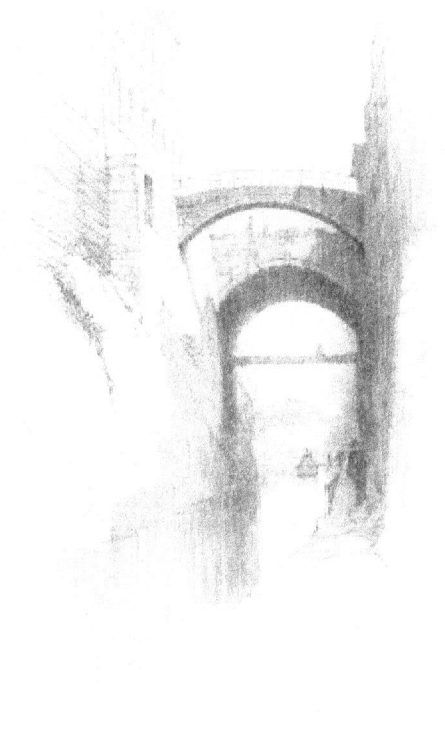

THE CANAL AND BRIDGE OF SIGHS.

THE WATER TOWER.

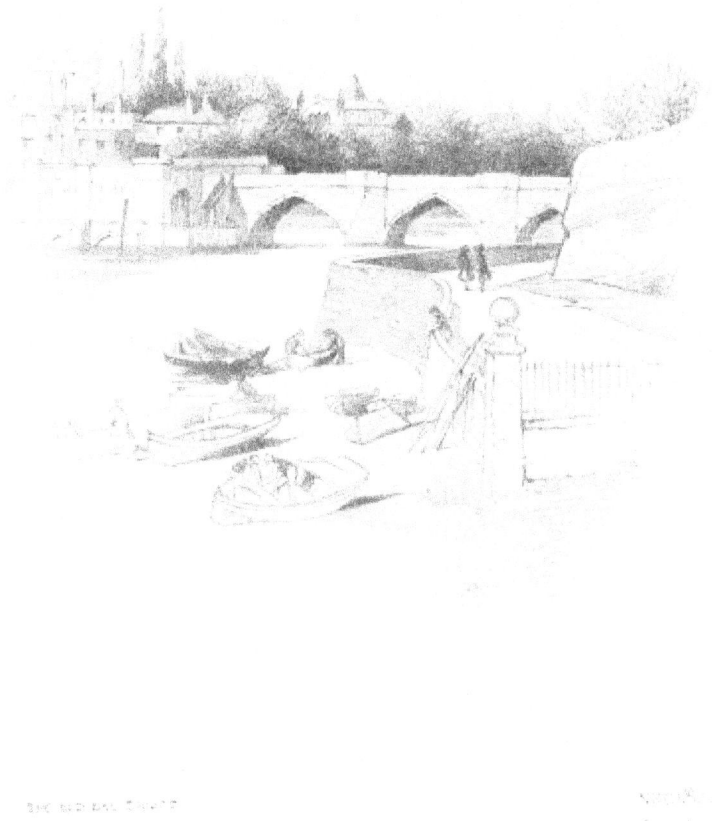

THE OLD DEE BRIDGE.

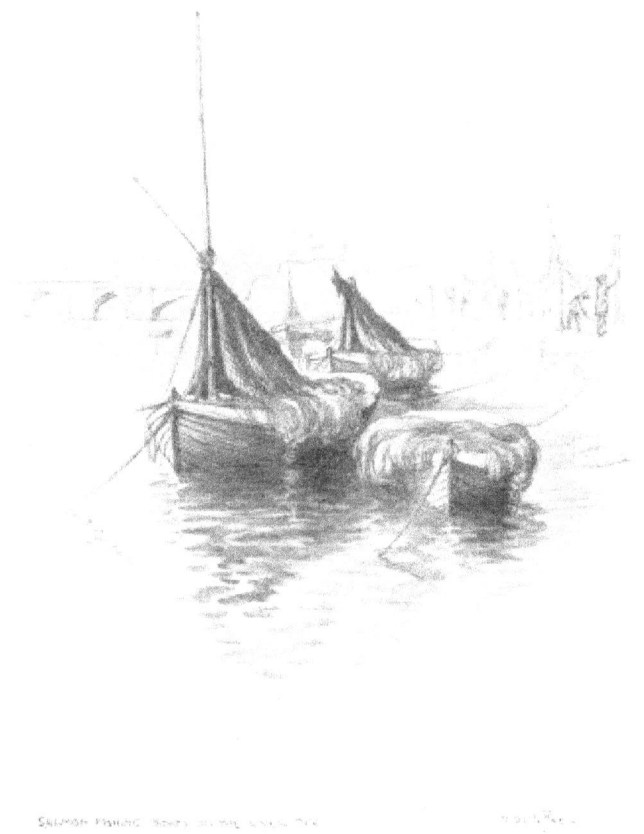

SALMON FISHING BOATS ON THE RIVER DEE.

SALMON FISHING BOATS
ON THE RIVER DEE.

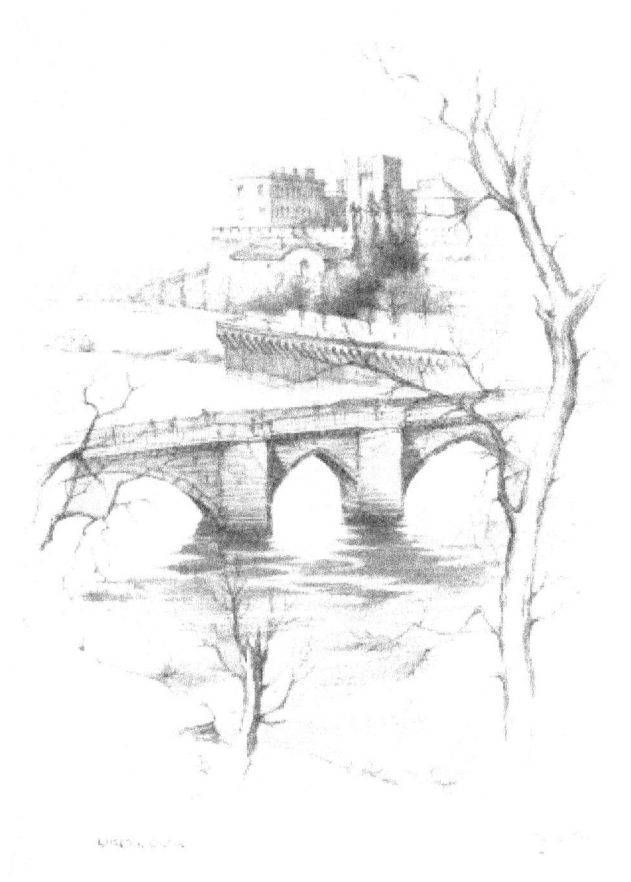

CHESTER CASTLE.

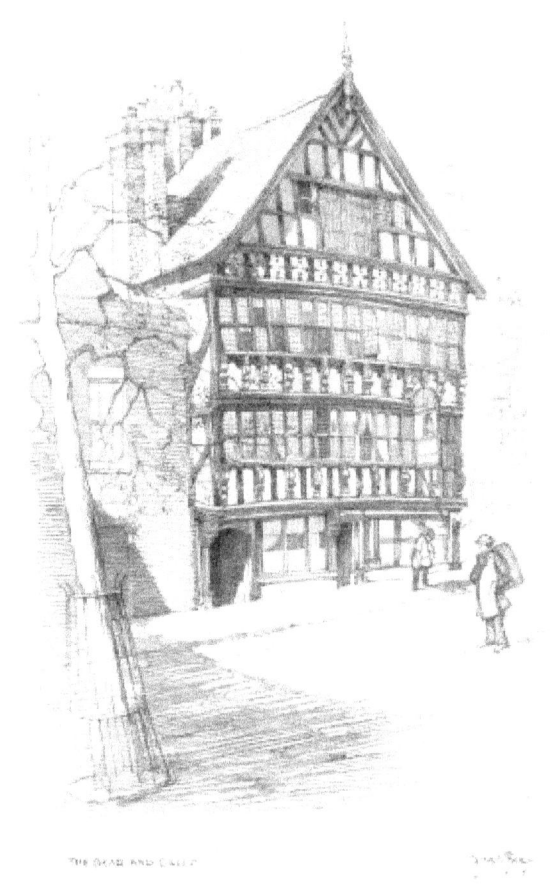

THE BEAR AND BILLET.

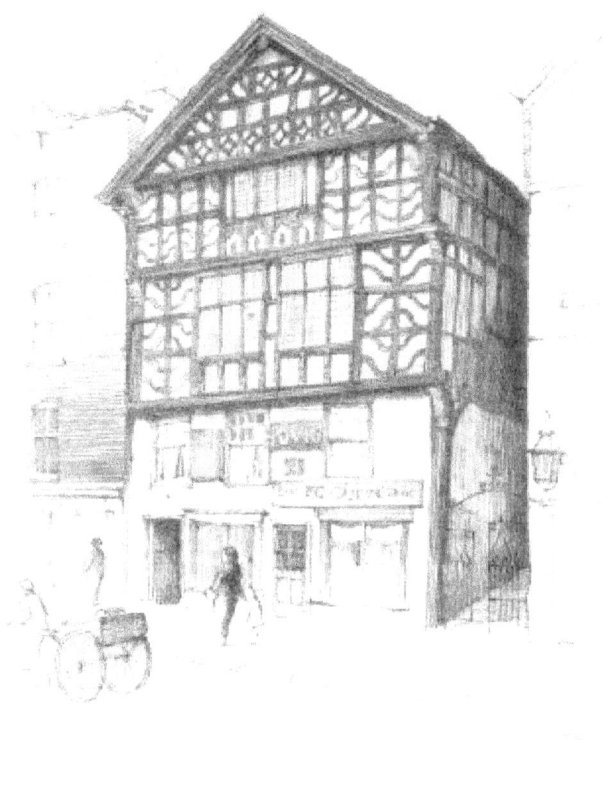

OLD HOUSE IN LOWER
BRIDGE STREET.

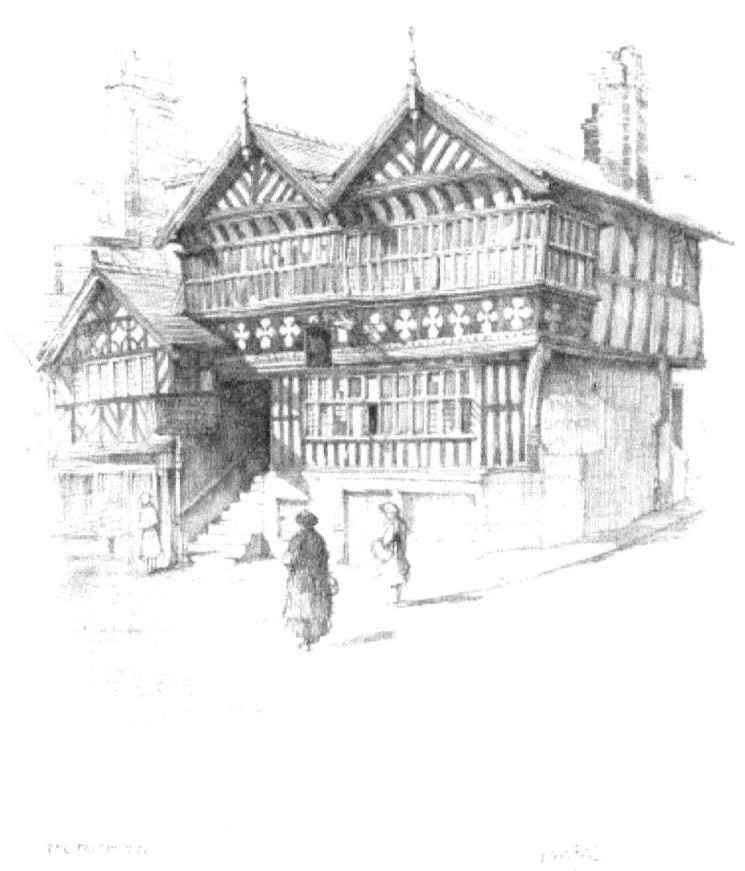

THE FALCON INN.

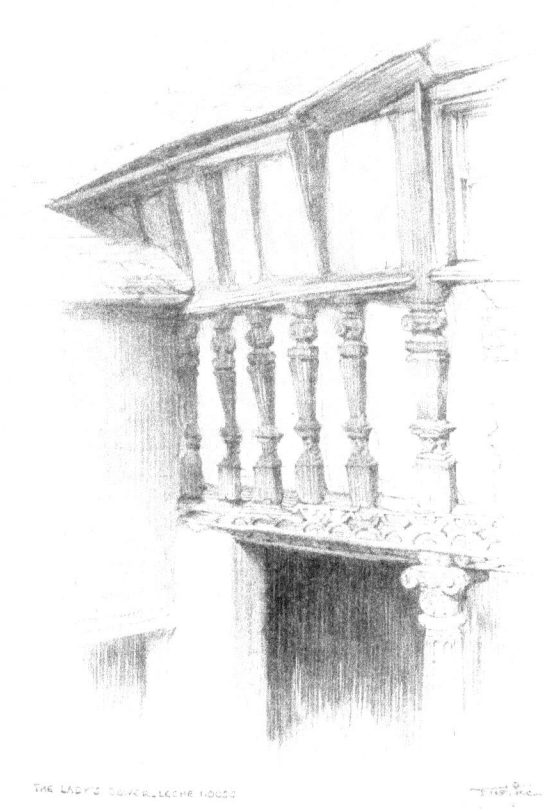

THE LADY'S BOWER, LECHE HOUSE.

THE LADY'S BOWER, LECHE HOUSE.

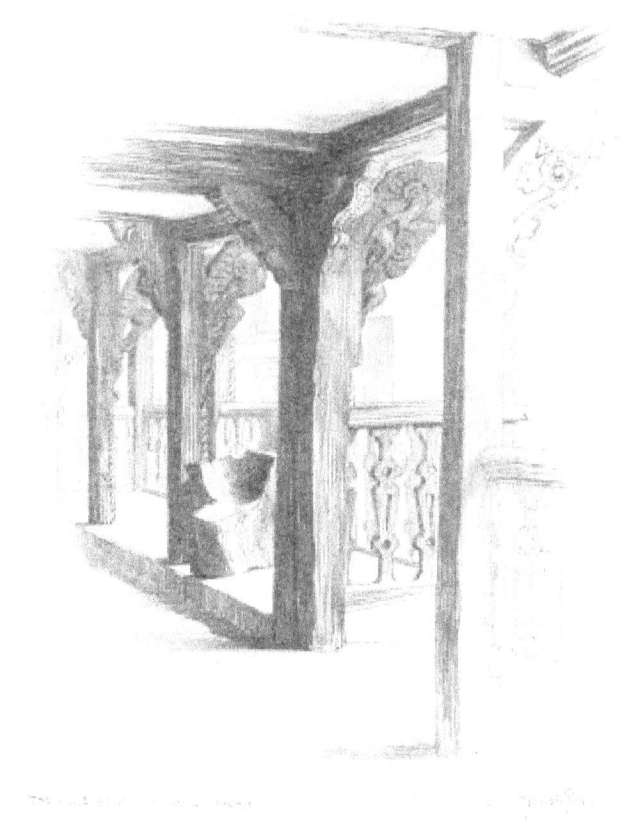

THE ROWS AT BISHOP LLOYD'S PALACE.

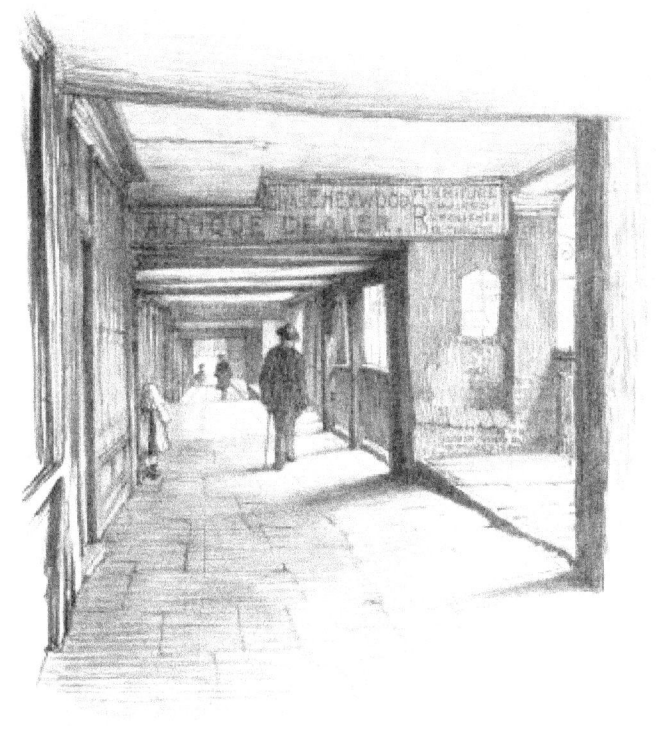

THE ROWS, WATERGATE STREET.

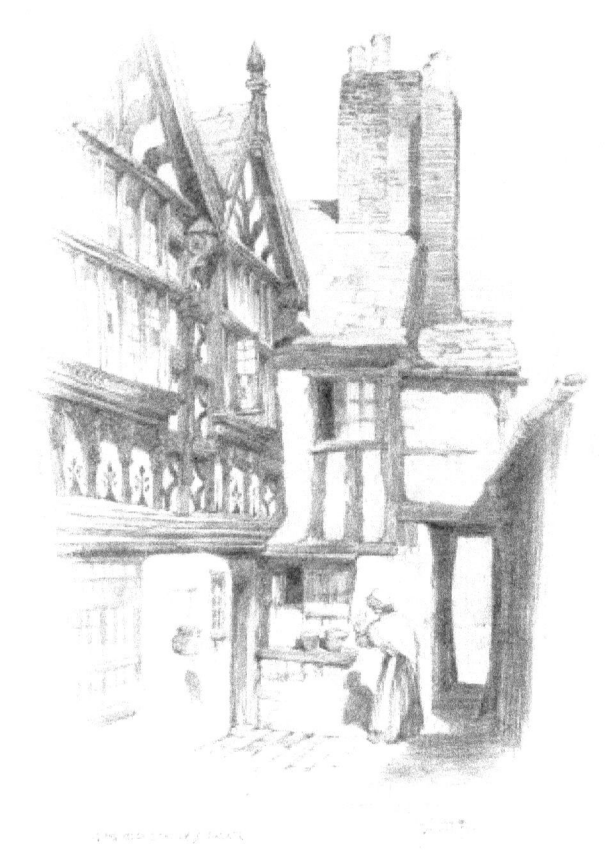

THE OLD STANLEY PALACE.

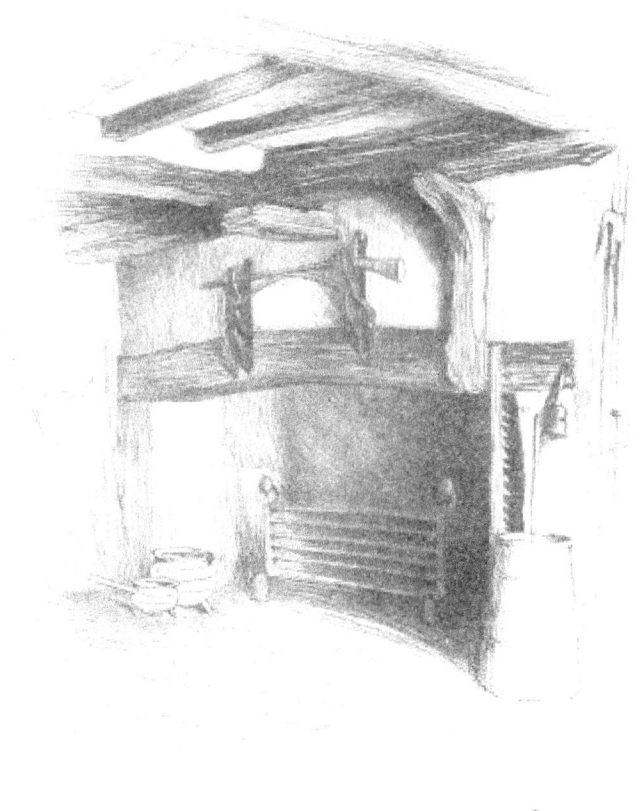

THE FIREPLACE AT
STANLEY PALACE.

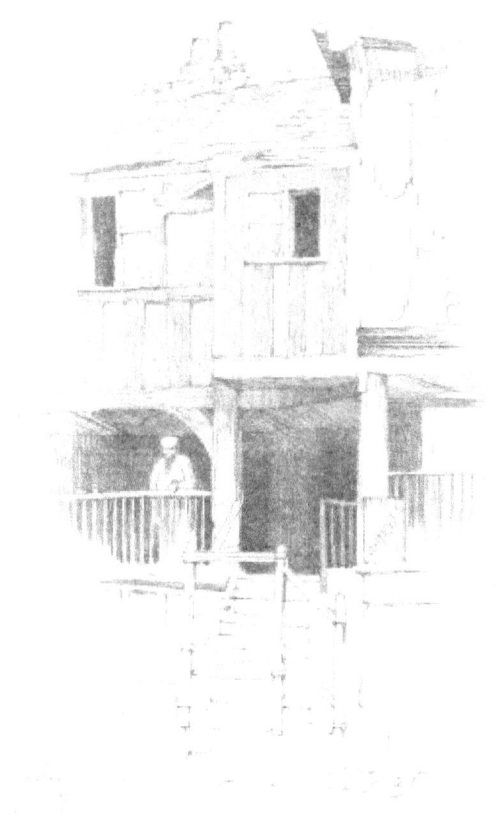

OLD HOUSES WATERGATE
Sᵀ "UNCLE TOM'S CABIN."

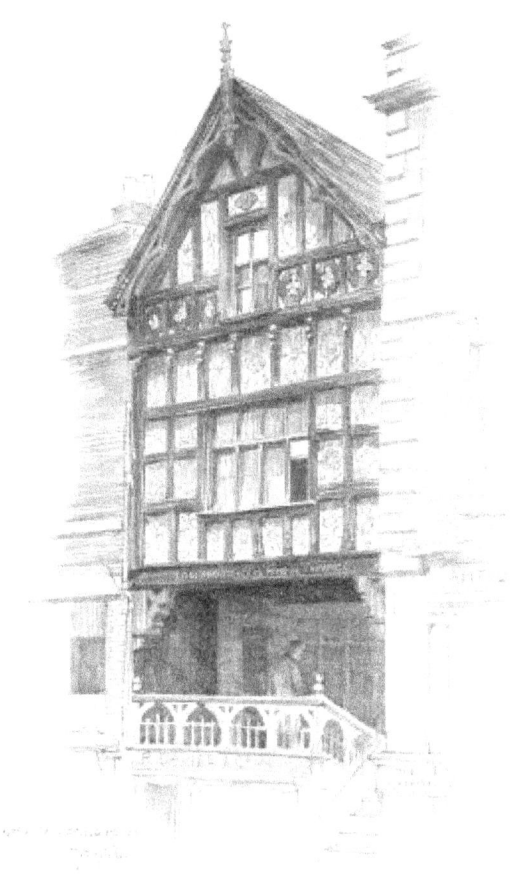

GOLD'S PROVIDENCE
HOUSE.

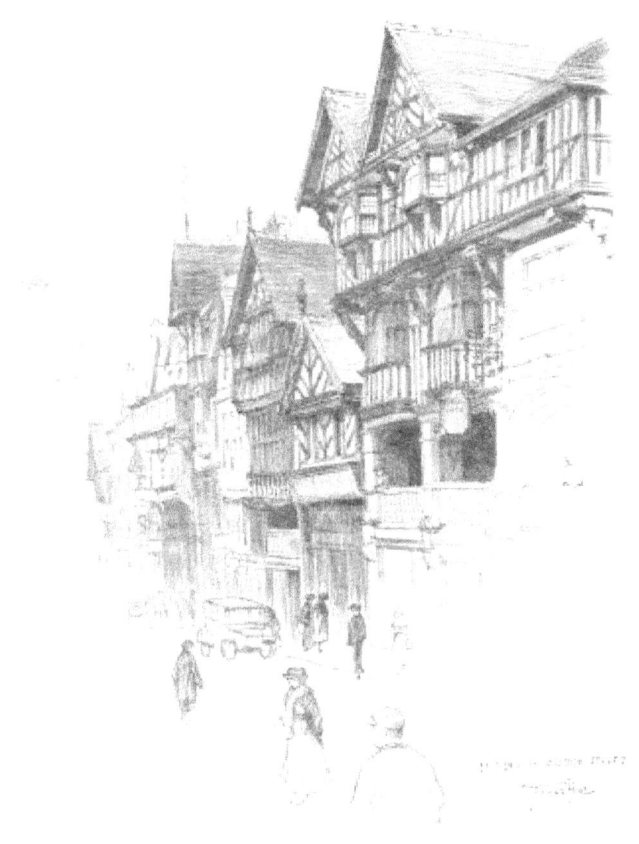

HOUSES IN BRIDGE STREET.

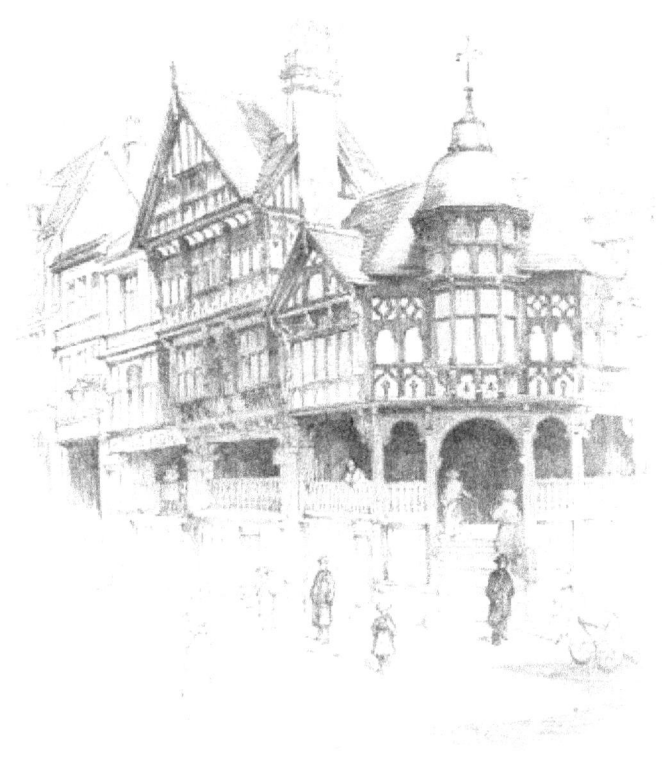

THE CROSS.

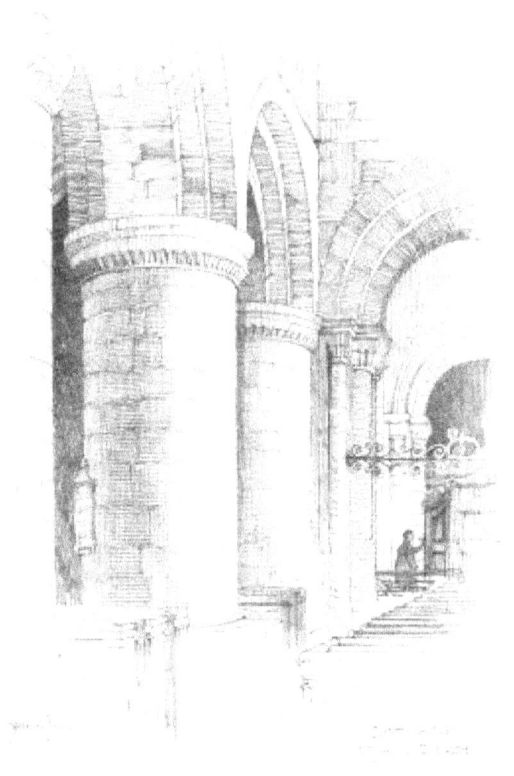

SOUTH AISLE S^T JOHN'S CHURCH.

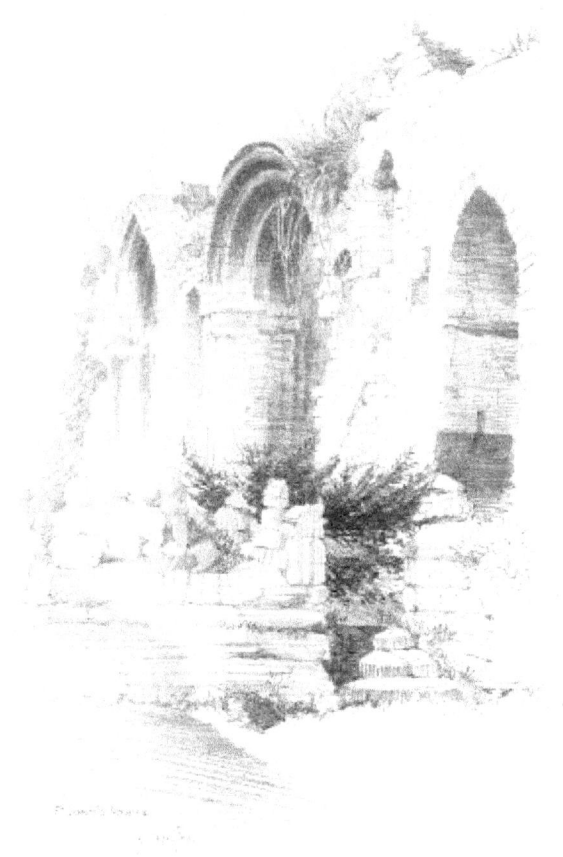

Sᵀ JOHN'S RUINS.

Ampleforth College

A Sketch-Book

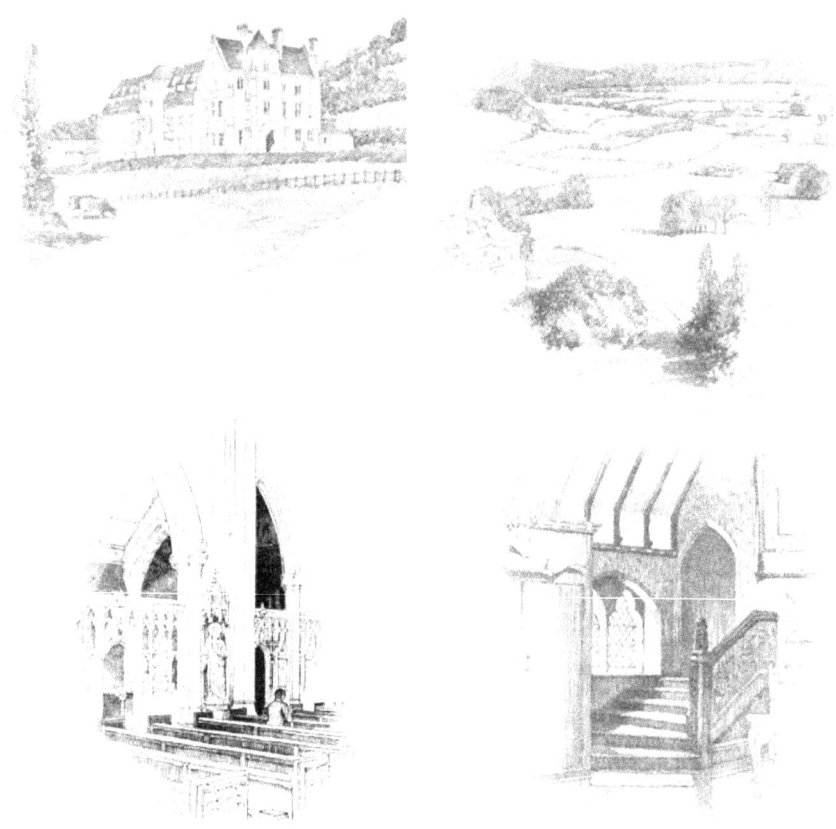

By Joseph Pike

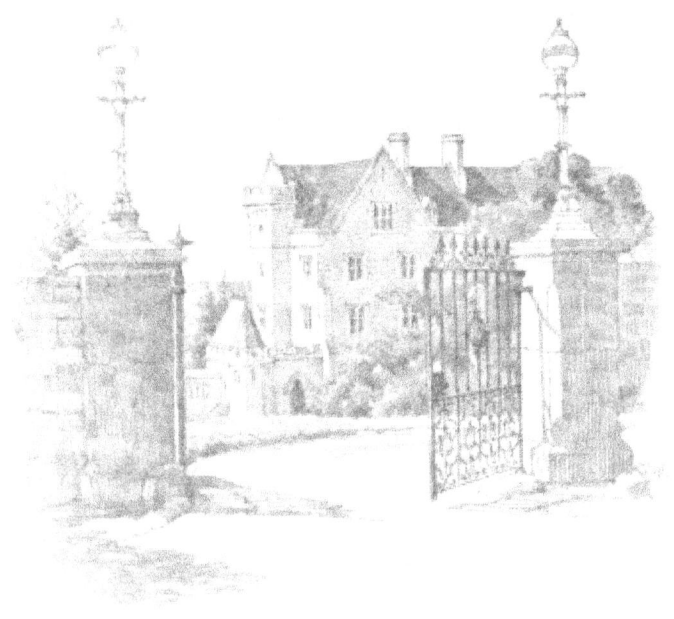

THE ENTRANCE GATES

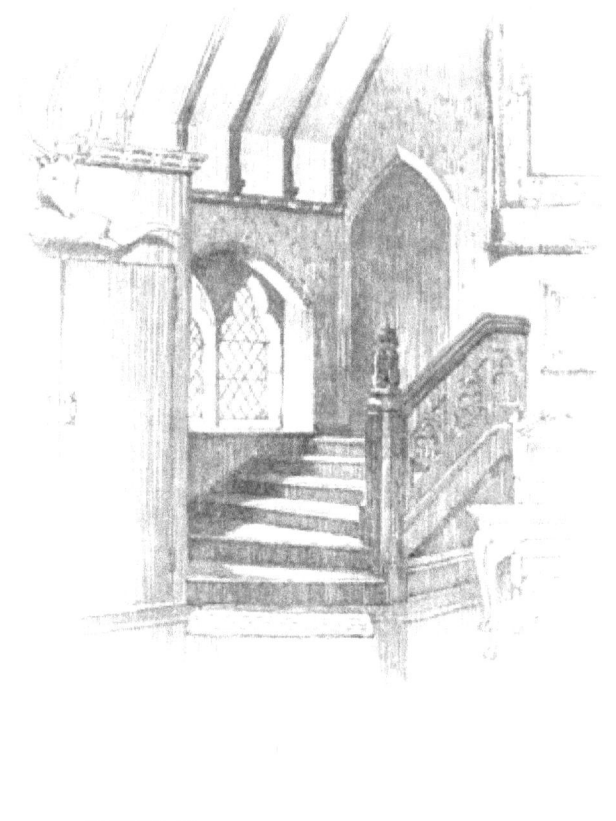

THE ENTRANCE HALL

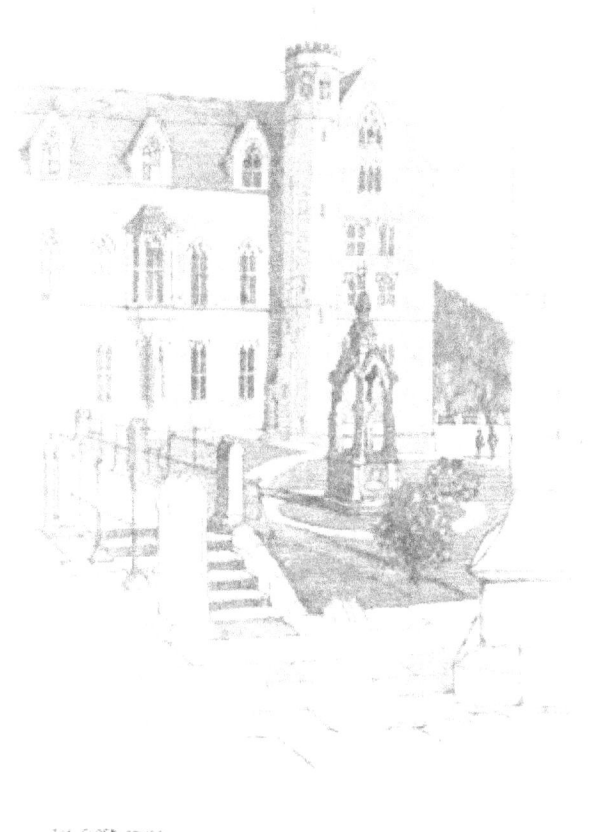

THE CLOCK TOWER

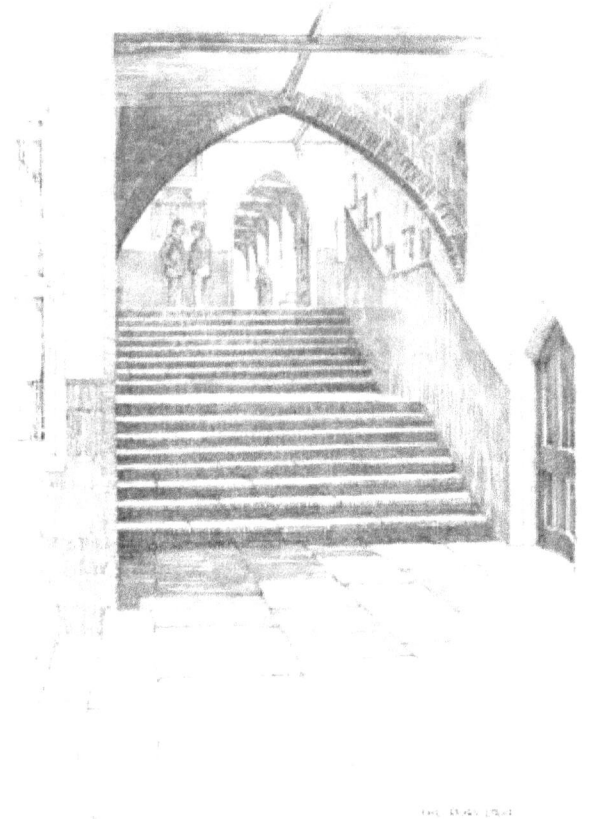

THE STUDY STEPS

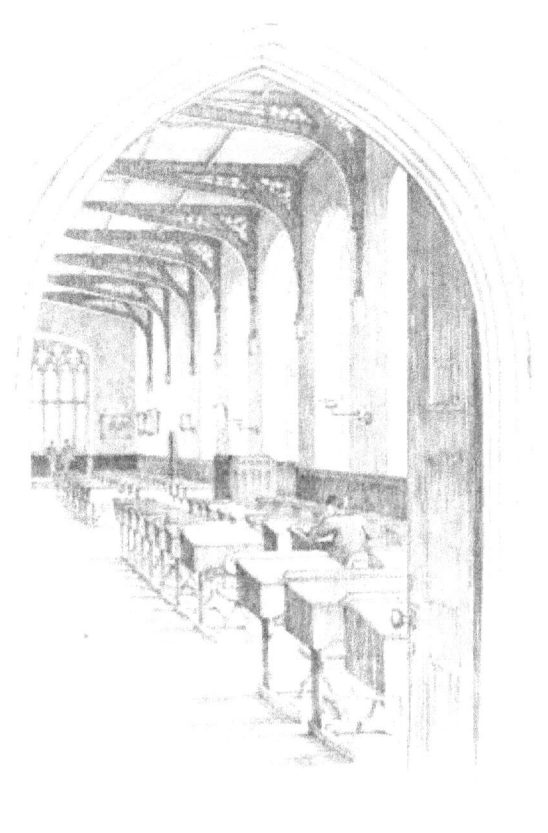

THE STUDY

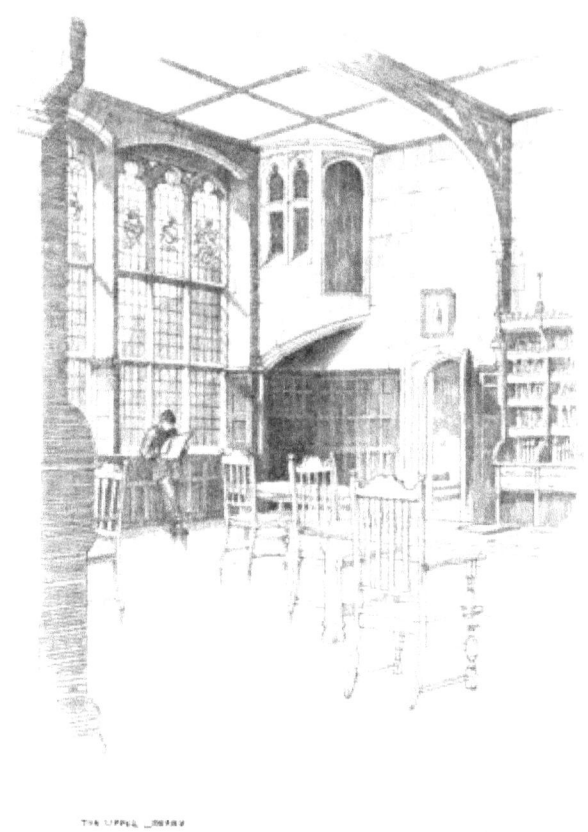

THE UPPER LIBRARY

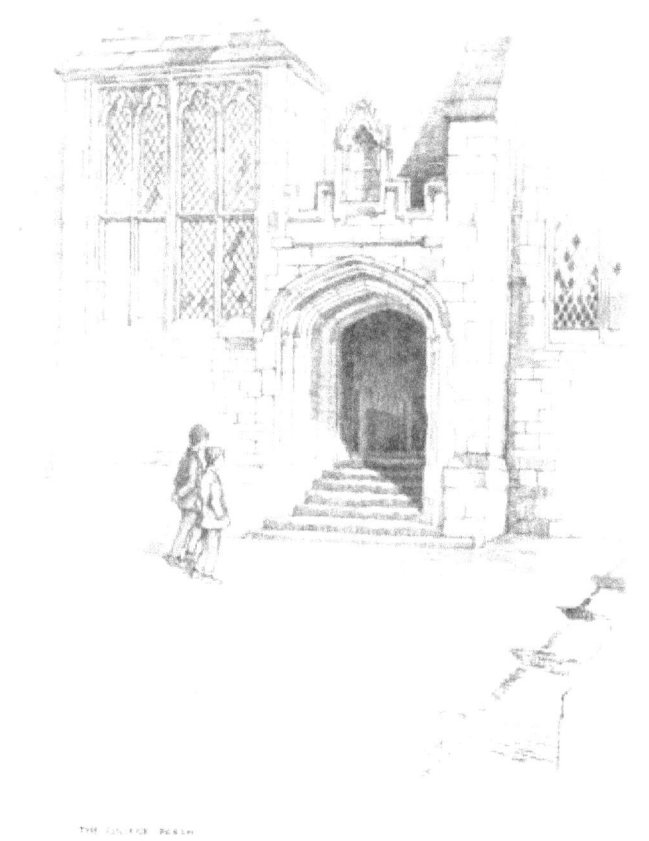

THE COLLEGE PORCH

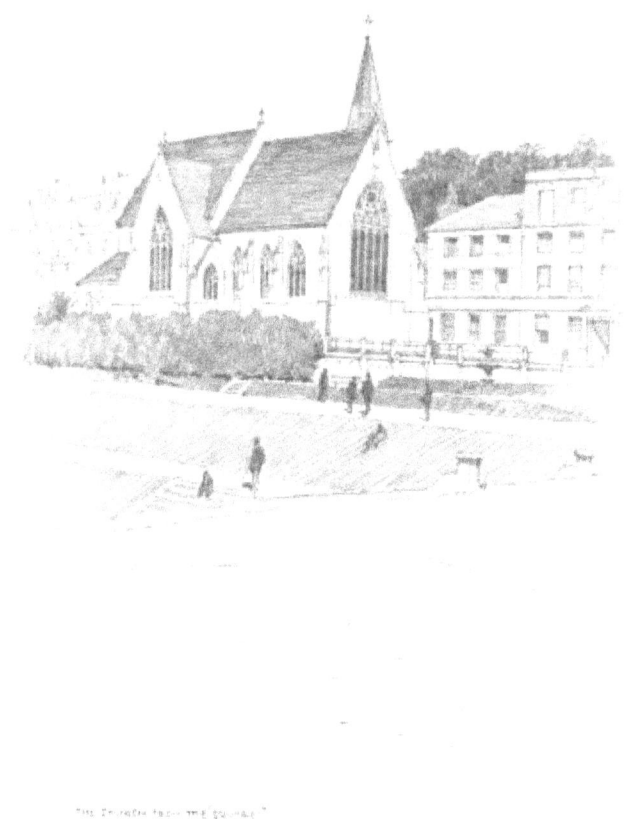

THE CHURCH FROM "THE SQUARE"

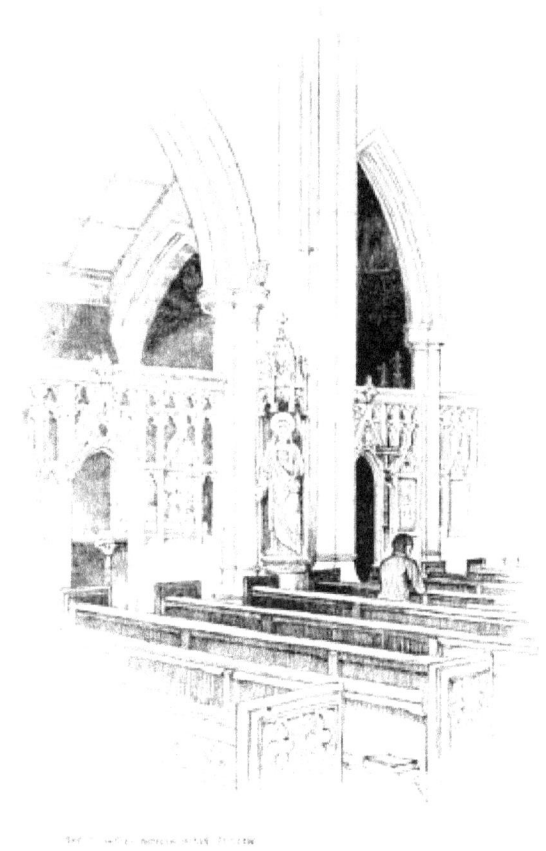

THE CHURCH —NORTH AISLE SCREEN

52

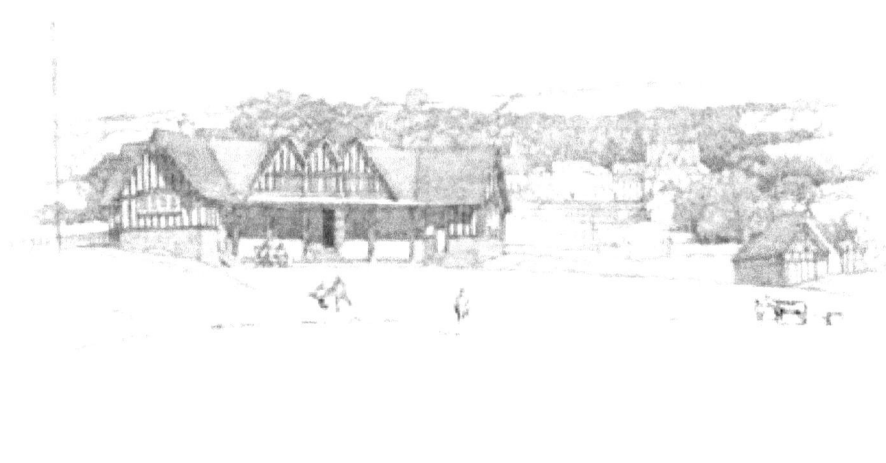

FROM THE CRICKET FIELD

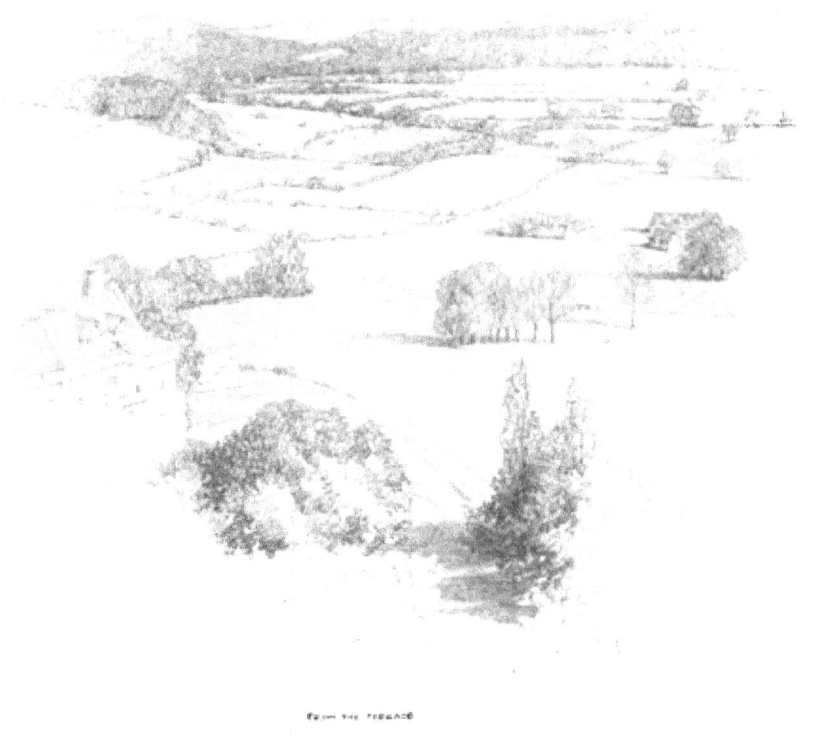

FROM THE TERRACE

FROM THE TERRACE

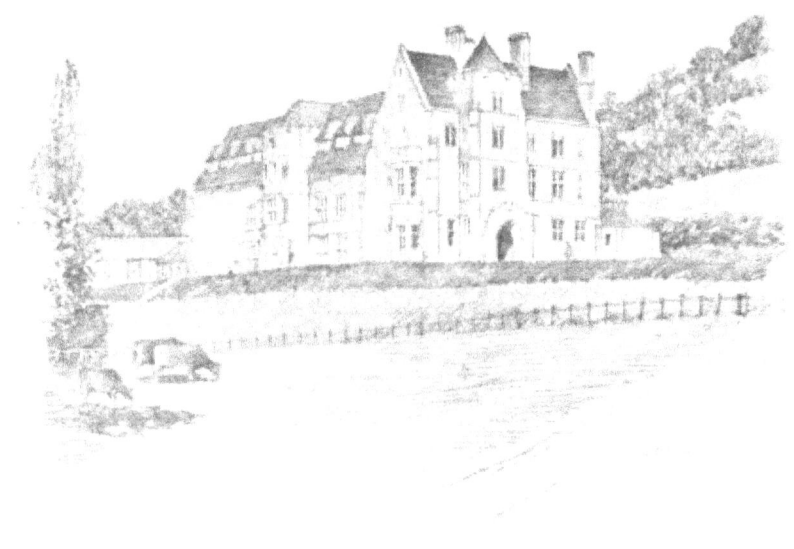

THE PREPARATORY SCHOOL

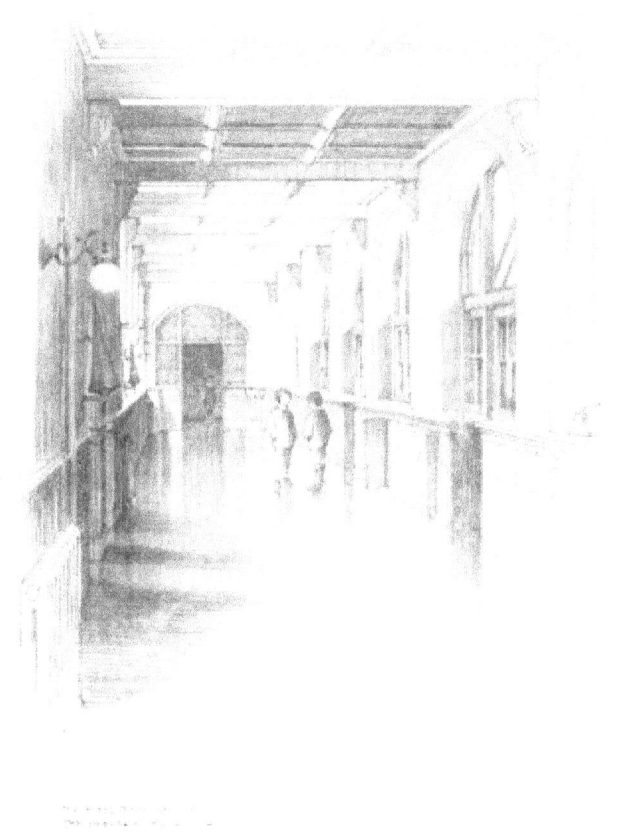

THE CLASS ROOM GALLERY—THE PREPARATORY SCHOOL

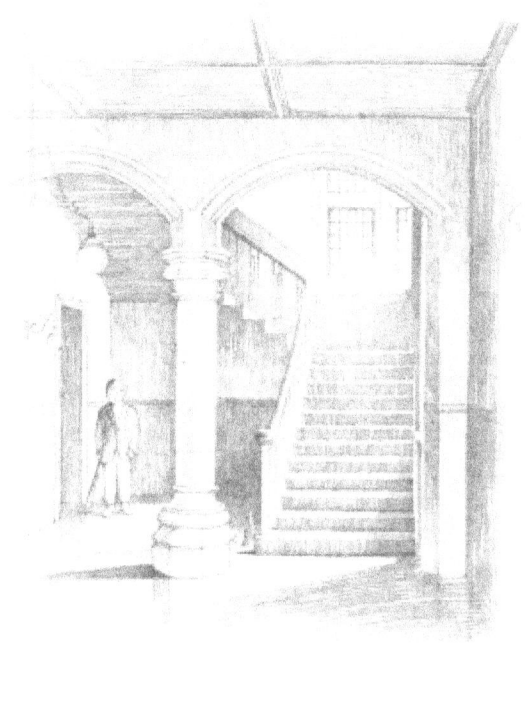

THE BOYS' ENTRANCE —THE PREPARATORY SCHOOL

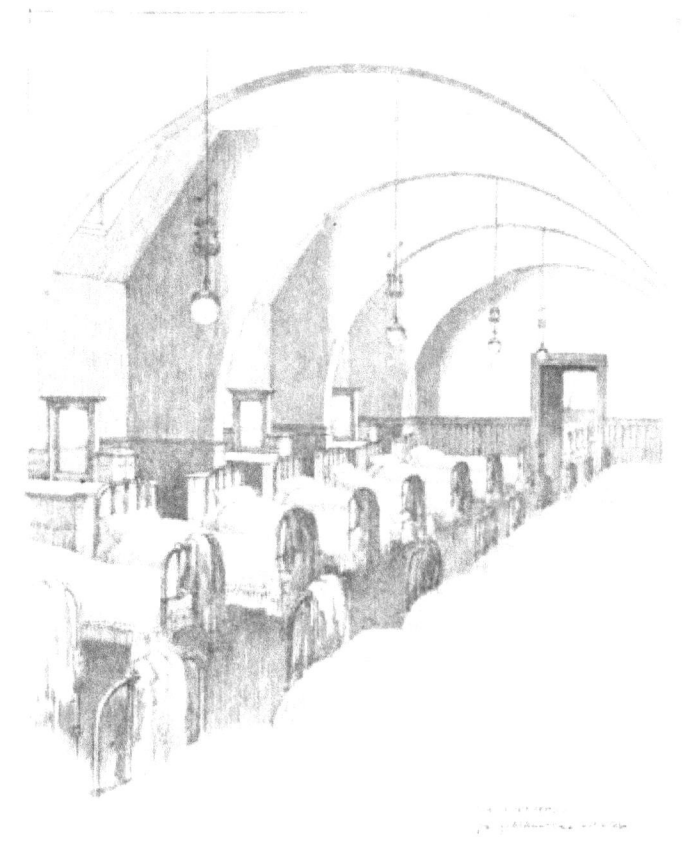

THE DORMITORY—THE PREPARATORY SCHOOL

www.ingramcontent.com/pod-product-compliance
Lightning Source LLC
Chambersburg PA
CBHW081259180526
45170CB00007B/2488